META QUEST 3 FOR EVERYONE: BEGINNERS TO EXPERTS

A COMPLETE GUIDE TO UNLOCKING IMMERSIVE
EXPERIENCES ACROSS ALL SKILL LEVELS

DAVID L. KESTER

DEDICATION

This book is dedicated to the explorers of the digital frontier, to those who dare to dream and venture beyond the limits of what we know. To the creators, the innovators, and the pioneers who push the boundaries of technology and imagination, this is for you. May your curiosity never wane, and may the virtual worlds you build continue to inspire, challenge, and transform all who experience them.

ACKNOWLEDGEMENT

I would like to extend my deepest gratitude to the entire Meta team, whose commitment to advancing virtual reality has made the Meta Quest 3 a groundbreaking and transformative device. Their dedication to innovation and their vision for the future of VR have inspired this work and countless others. I am also incredibly grateful to the developers, content creators, and the vibrant Meta community, whose creativity and collaboration continue to shape the immersive experiences we now have at our fingertips.

A special thanks goes to my family and friends, whose unwavering support and encouragement have been my guiding light throughout this journey. Their belief in this project kept me grounded and motivated, even during the most challenging moments. Additionally, I would like to express my appreciation to my readers, whose enthusiasm and passion for virtual reality have made writing this book such a rewarding experience. Thank you all for being part of this adventure.

TABLE OF CONTENT

PROLOGUE

Virtual reality (VR) has transformed from a distant dream of science fiction into a tangible, immersive experience that is reshaping how we interact with the digital world. The journey of VR began decades ago, rooted in the aspirations of innovators who imagined a world where technology could transcend the boundaries of physical space. Early prototypes, such as the Sensorama in the 1960s, laid the groundwork for the concept of immersive environments. These machines, though primitive by today's standards, were revolutionary in their ambition to engage multiple senses simultaneously. As technology advanced, the 1980s and 1990s brought notable milestones, including the introduction of head-mounted displays and rudimentary motion tracking. Companies like Sega and Nintendo attempted to bring VR to the masses, but technological limitations and high costs relegated these efforts to niche markets.

The 21st century marked a turning point for VR with the advent of more sophisticated computing power, compact hardware, and increased investment in research and development. Oculus, with its Rift headset in 2012, spearheaded the modern VR renaissance, capturing the imagination of both developers and consumers. By 2014, when Facebook acquired Oculus, it became clear that VR was no longer a fleeting trend but a paradigm shift in digital interaction. Since then, VR has evolved rapidly, encompassing applications far beyond gaming, including education, healthcare, and professional training. At the forefront of this evolution stands Meta, the company formerly known as Facebook, which has consistently pushed the boundaries of what VR can achieve.

Meta's contributions to the VR landscape have been transformative, driven by a vision to create interconnected virtual spaces where people can work, play, and socialize. The introduction of the Meta Quest series marked a pivotal moment in making VR accessible to a broader audience. Unlike earlier systems that required expensive, high-powered PCs or external sensors, Meta Quest offered a standalone solution with the freedom to move untethered. With each iteration, Meta refined its technology, blending cutting-edge hardware with an intuitive user experience.

The Meta Quest 3 represents the culmination of years of innovation. It stands as a testament to Meta's commitment to revolutionizing the VR experience. Equipped with a powerful Snapdragon XR2 Gen 2 processor, high-resolution displays, and enhanced mixed reality capabilities, the Quest 3 redefines what's possible in immersive technology. It offers users the ability to seamlessly transition between augmented reality (AR) and VR, creating a hybrid experience that blurs the lines between the physical and digital worlds. For gamers, this means richer, more interactive environments; for professionals, it opens doors to virtual collaboration and advanced training simulations; and for creatives, it becomes a tool for designing, building, and storytelling in three dimensions.

This book is designed to guide you through every aspect of the Meta Quest 3, making it approachable for both newcomers and seasoned VR enthusiasts. Whether you are a gamer eager to explore the latest titles, a professional seeking innovative solution, or simply a tech enthusiast curious about the future of digital interaction, this book has something for you. It breaks down the complexities of the device into clear, actionable insights, ensuring you can unlock its full potential.

To navigate this journey, this book is structured to cater to a wide audience. The initial chapters introduce you to the Meta Quest 3's hardware and basic functionalities, ensuring a smooth onboarding experience. As you progress, you will delve deeper into advanced features, tips, and tricks to enhance your immersion. For developers and creators, dedicated sections explore the tools and opportunities for building within the Meta ecosystem. Finally, we will reflect on the broader implications of VR and the role of Meta Quest 3 in shaping the future.

By the time you reach the end of this book, you will not only understand the Meta Quest 3 but also appreciate the larger narrative of VR's evolution and its boundless possibilities. This is more than a guide; it's an invitation to join a revolution in how we experience and interact with the world around us. Welcome to the future of virtual reality.

CHAPTER 1: GETTING STARTED WITH META QUEST 3

The anticipation of unboxing a new device is a thrilling experience, and with the Meta Quest 3, that excitement is only heightened by the promise of groundbreaking technology. As you open the sleek, well-designed packaging, you are greeted by the headset, controllers, and essential accessories, each meticulously arranged to convey both functionality and elegance. The first impression is one of quality and innovation, a testament to Meta's commitment to delivering a premium product. Alongside the hardware, you'll find a quick start guide, safety information, and charging cables, all neatly tucked away to ensure your unboxing process is as seamless as possible.

From the moment you hold the Quest 3 headset, its lightweight design and ergonomic build stand out. The high-quality materials provide a sense of durability, while the streamlined contours promise a comfortable fit for extended use. The controllers, now redesigned with enhanced tracking capabilities, feel intuitive and responsive in your hands. As you lay out the components, the possibilities of what this device can offer begin to unfold.

The Meta Quest 3 isn't just a collection of hardware; it's a gateway to immersive experiences that redefine how you interact with digital content. The headset is the centerpiece, featuring advanced displays that deliver crisp visuals with vibrant colors and sharp contrasts. Its compact form factor houses cutting-edge sensors and cameras, enabling features like passthrough, which allows you to see your physical surroundings without removing the headset. This is complemented by eye-tracking technology that enhances interaction and ensures a more intuitive user experience.

The controllers are equally impressive, designed with comfort and functionality in mind. Their precise motion tracking and adaptive triggers offer an unparalleled level of control, making even the most complex tasks feel natural. Additionally, Meta offers a range of optional accessories, including enhanced head straps for improved comfort and charging docks to keep your devices powered and ready.

Setting up your Meta Quest 3 is a straightforward process, designed to get you into the virtual world quickly and effortlessly. Begin by ensuring the headset and controllers are fully charged using the provided cables. Once powered on, you'll be guided through a series of on-screen prompts that walk you through the initial setup. The intuitive interface simplifies tasks like connecting to Wi-Fi, pairing the controllers, and adjusting the headset for optimal fit and clarity.

One of the first steps is creating or logging into your Meta account, a necessary gateway to accessing the Quest ecosystem. This account serves as the hub for your games, apps, and social interactions, seamlessly integrating all your virtual experiences. After logging in, the device will check for software updates, ensuring you have the latest features and enhancements.

As you complete the setup process, you'll be prompted to define your play area using the Guardian system. This innovative feature uses the headset's cameras to map your physical surroundings, allowing you to draw boundaries that keep you safe while immersed in VR. The Guardian system adapts to different environments, whether you're in a spacious living room or a cozy corner, ensuring you can enjoy the Quest 3 with confidence.

The initial setup also introduces you to the passthrough mode, a feature that allows you to view your real-world surroundings in grayscale through the headset's cameras. This capability is invaluable for situational awareness, enabling you to seamlessly switch between virtual and physical realities without removing the headset. The combination of passthrough and eye-tracking technology creates a seamless integration of the physical and digital worlds, making the Meta Quest 3 not just a VR device but a mixed-reality powerhouse.

By the time you complete the setup, you'll be ready to dive into the Meta Quest ecosystem, a world of limitless possibilities. From the unboxing to the initial configuration, every aspect of getting started with the Meta Quest 3 is designed to be intuitive and user-friendly, ensuring that even those new to VR can embark on their journey with ease. This is just the beginning of your exploration into a realm where the boundaries of reality are redefined, and the possibilities are only limited by your imagination.

CHAPTER 2: THE TECHNOLOGY BEHIND THE MAGIC

The Meta Quest 3 represents a significant leap forward in virtual reality technology, combining cutting-edge hardware with innovative features to deliver a seamless and immersive experience. At the heart of this device lies the Snapdragon XR2 Gen 2 processor, a powerful chip specifically designed for extended reality (XR) applications. This processor is not only faster but also more efficient than its predecessor, enabling the Quest 3 to handle complex computations, high-resolution graphics, and real-time tracking with remarkable ease. Paired with advanced lenses and high-resolution displays, the Quest 3 offers visuals that are both sharper and more vibrant, setting a new standard for clarity and realism in VR.

The displays on the Meta Quest 3 are engineered to enhance immersion, with improved pixel density and refresh rates that minimize motion blur and provide a smoother visual experience. The lenses have also been redesigned to reduce the "screen door effect," a common issue in earlier VR headsets where users could see the gaps between pixels. This innovation ensures that the virtual worlds you explore feel more lifelike and engaging, allowing you to lose yourself in the experience without distractions.

When compared to previous models like the Meta Quest 2, the Quest 3 showcases significant advancements in nearly every aspect. The XR2 Gen 2 processor delivers a noticeable performance boost, enabling more complex and interactive experiences. The inclusion of color passthrough technology, a feature absent in earlier versions, transforms the Quest 3 into a true mixed-reality device, seamlessly blending the virtual and physical worlds. Additionally, the improved ergonomic design and lighter weight make it more comfortable for extended use, further enhancing the overall user experience.

One of the standout features of the Meta Quest 3 is its integration of augmented reality (AR) and virtual reality (VR) capabilities. This dual functionality is made possible by advanced external cameras and sensors that capture and interpret your surroundings in real-time. With color passthrough technology, you can see a vivid representation of your physical environment while interacting with virtual objects overlaid onto it. This opens up a world of possibilities, from playing games that incorporate your actual living room to designing virtual furniture and seeing how it fits in your space before making a purchase.

The mixed-reality capabilities of the Quest 3 also have practical applications beyond entertainment. For professionals, it provides tools for remote collaboration, allowing teams to meet in virtual spaces while remaining grounded in their physical environments. Educators can create interactive lessons that combine real-world elements with virtual enhancements, offering students a unique and engaging way to learn. Even daily tasks, such as fitness routines or home organization, can be elevated with the integration of AR and VR, making the Quest 3 a versatile tool for a wide range of activities.

Central to the Quest 3 experience is its intuitive operating system, which has been designed to make navigation and customization effortless. The user interface is clean and straightforward, ensuring that both beginners and seasoned VR users can quickly find their way around. From the home screen, you can access your library of apps, games, and experiences, as well as adjust settings to personalize your device. The system supports voice commands, allowing you to control various functions hands-free, adding an extra layer of convenience.

Customization options on the Quest 3 are extensive, enabling users to tailor their experience to suit their preferences. You can adjust visual settings like brightness and contrast to optimize the display for different lighting conditions. The controllers and headset can be mapped and configured to meet specific needs, ensuring that the device feels as natural and responsive as possible. Additionally, the ability to create virtual spaces, such as custom home environments or workstations, allows for a more personalized and immersive experience.

The Quest operating system also supports seamless updates, ensuring that your device stays current with the latest features and improvements. These updates often include enhancements to performance, new tools for developers, and additional functionality that expands the capabilities of the headset. Meta's commitment to continuous improvement ensures that the Quest 3 remains a cutting-edge device throughout its lifecycle, providing users with ongoing value and innovation.

By combining state-of-the-art hardware, mixed-reality features, and a user-friendly operating system, the Meta Quest 3 has redefined what a standalone VR headset can achieve. It is not just a device but a platform that bridges the gap between the physical and digital worlds, offering endless possibilities for exploration, creativity, and connection. With its advanced technology and thoughtful design, the Quest 3 invites users to step into a new era of immersive experiences where the only limit is their imagination.

CHAPTER 3: NAVIGATING THE META QUEST ECOSYSTEM

The Meta Quest ecosystem is an expansive network designed to provide users with seamless access to apps, games, and social experiences. At its core is the Meta Store, the digital hub where everything begins. Accessible directly through the headset or via a companion app on your smartphone or tablet, the Meta Store offers a vast library of content tailored to all interests and skill levels. Whether you're looking for immersive gaming adventures, creative tools, or productivity apps, the store is the gateway to endless possibilities.

Navigating the Meta Store is intuitive, with categories that make it easy to find what you're looking for. From trending games to curated collections, the platform ensures that new users and veterans alike can quickly discover content that suits their tastes. Each listing provides detailed descriptions, user reviews, and ratings, helping you make informed decisions before downloading. With just a few clicks, you can install apps directly onto your Quest 3, ready to dive into new worlds at a moment's notice.

In addition to free apps and games, the Meta Store also offers premium content that can be purchased individually or accessed through subscriptions. Subscriptions like Meta Quest+ provide added value, granting users access to exclusive perks and a rotating selection of top-tier titles each month. For a small monthly fee, this service allows you to explore premium content without committing to full purchases, making it an excellent option for those who want to sample a variety of experiences.

Meta Quest+ isn't just about games; it often includes unique apps and features that cater to different interests. Whether you're into fitness, meditation, or exploring virtual art galleries, the subscription unlocks opportunities to enhance your VR journey. Additionally, members often receive discounts on popular titles, making it a cost-effective way to expand your library. Meta ensures that its subscription services evolve over time, adding new benefits to keep users engaged and excited about their membership.

One of the standout features of the Meta Quest ecosystem is its emphasis on social connectivity. At its core, VR is about more than just individual experiences—it's about bringing people together in ways that transcend physical boundaries.

The Quest 3 excels in this area, offering a range of tools and features designed to foster interaction and collaboration.

Multiplayer gaming is one of the most popular ways users connect within the Meta community. From competitive battles to cooperative adventures, multiplayer games on the Quest 3 create opportunities to bond with friends and meet new people from around the world. Games often include voice chat and customizable avatars, allowing players to communicate and express themselves in unique ways.

Beyond gaming, the Meta ecosystem provides virtual hangout spaces where users can socialize, attend events, or simply relax together. Apps like Horizon Worlds offer expansive virtual environments where you can interact with others, participate in activities, or even create your own spaces. Whether you're hosting a virtual movie night, attending a live concert, or exploring an art exhibit, these shared experiences make VR a powerful tool for building connections.

Meta has also integrated social features directly into the Quest 3's operating system, making it easy to stay connected while immersed in VR. You can send messages, share content, and join friends in apps with just a few clicks. Notifications ensure you never miss an invitation or update, keeping you in the loop without disrupting your experience.

The sense of community extends to developer and creator collaborations, as Meta fosters an ecosystem where users can contribute their own creations to the platform. Whether it's designing custom worlds, building new apps, or sharing artistic projects, the Quest ecosystem encourages innovation and creativity. These contributions not only enrich the platform but also provide opportunities for creators to monetize their work, turning their passion into a sustainable endeavor.

The Meta Quest ecosystem is more than just a collection of apps and features; it's a dynamic, interconnected platform that evolves with its users. By prioritizing accessibility, personalization, and social interaction, Meta has created a space where everyone can find something to enjoy. Whether you're downloading your first game, subscribing to Quest+, or connecting with others in virtual worlds, the Quest 3 ensures that your journey through VR is as engaging and rewarding as possible.

CHAPTER 4: UNLOCKING GAMING POTENTIAL

The Meta Quest 3 opens up a world of gaming experiences, ranging from simple, intuitive games for beginners to deep, complex titles for seasoned VR veterans. For newcomers to VR, the transition into this immersive world can be both exciting and overwhelming. Fortunately, the platform offers a wide range of user-friendly games designed to ease players into the virtual reality experience without the steep learning curve often associated with traditional gaming.

Top games for beginners include a variety of genres, from casual puzzle games to light action-packed adventures, making it easy for players to find something that suits their comfort level. Titles like Beat Saber, for instance, are perfect for newcomers. Its simple premise—slice through colorful blocks in rhythm with the music—makes it accessible to anyone, regardless of experience. The controls are easy to grasp, the gameplay is fun and energetic, and it offers a satisfying sense of progression as you unlock new songs and difficulty levels. Similarly, Fruit Ninja VR takes the familiar mobile game and brings it into the virtual world with simple mechanics that anyone can enjoy. These games focus on fun, movement, and a light touch of challenge, ideal for people just getting their feet wet in the world of VR.

For those interested in exploring more in-depth adventures, The Climb 2 offers an introduction to a more immersive environment. It combines beautiful scenery with engaging mechanics like rock climbing, providing a fresh challenge without overwhelming newcomers. Additionally, Moss introduces players to a charming world where they control a small mouse named Quill, navigating puzzles and platforming challenges. Its third-person perspective and slower pace make it less intense but still captivating. These titles introduce beginners to the possibilities of VR without demanding expert skills or prior knowledge.

Once you've grown accustomed to the mechanics and movement of VR, you might want to dive into more advanced gaming experiences that take full advantage of the Meta Quest 3's capabilities. For VR veterans looking for challenges and intricate narratives, the library of advanced games is nothing short of impressive. These titles push the limits of what VR can offer, providing expansive worlds, complex mechanics, and experiences that require not just skill, but strategic thinking and perseverance.

One such title is Half-Life: Alyx, a game that has set the bar for VR shooters. Set in the legendary Half-Life universe, the game combines stunning visuals with deep storytelling and mechanics that require players to physically interact with the environment. The ability to manipulate objects, solve puzzles, and engage in combat with precision makes it a must-play for any VR enthusiast. Star Wars: Squadrons is another great example for veterans, offering a fully immersive space combat experience where you can pilot iconic Star Wars ships and participate in intense dogfights. The combination of immersive VR mechanics and the franchise's fan-favorite setting makes it a thrilling, action-packed experience for those seeking advanced gameplay.

For players seeking a truly immersive simulation experience, The Walking Dead: Saints & Sinners is a standout. This game challenges players to survive a zombie apocalypse, offering visceral combat, realistic weapon handling, and a richly detailed world. It's a far cry from casual VR gaming, demanding focus and quick reflexes as players navigate a terrifying world filled with danger at every turn. Similarly, No Man's Sky VR brings the expansive universe of No Man's Sky to the Quest 3, allowing players to explore planets, engage in space battles, and mine resources, all in a vast, procedurally generated galaxy. These titles require a high level of commitment and familiarity with VR gaming, making them perfect for those looking to challenge themselves in a more immersive setting.

While VR gaming offers endless possibilities, it's important to optimize your experience for comfort and performance. One of the most common concerns new players face in VR is motion sickness, but there are several tips and adjustments you can make to minimize this issue. First, adjusting the fit of the headset to ensure it sits comfortably on your face is crucial. A secure, balanced fit prevents unnecessary movement of the lenses, reducing the likelihood of discomfort. Additionally, many games offer comfort settings, such as reducing the field of view or enabling a smooth movement option instead of teleporting, which can ease the onset of motion sickness.

If you're looking to get the most out of your graphics, adjusting the settings to match your play environment is key. While the Quest 3 offers excellent graphical performance, settings such as brightness, contrast, and refresh rates can be fine-tuned for each game. Play around with these options to find what works best for your personal preferences and lighting conditions. Many users find that reducing the overall graphical intensity in certain demanding games can help improve performance, ensuring a smooth and enjoyable experience without lag or stuttering.

Battery life is another factor to consider when optimizing your gaming experience. While the Quest 3 offers decent battery life, long gaming sessions can drain the power quickly. To extend battery life, turn off unnecessary features like Wi-Fi or Bluetooth if you're not using them, and reduce the screen brightness. Additionally, utilizing the charging dock and ensuring your headset is fully charged between sessions will help you avoid interruptions during gameplay. For extended gaming, consider investing in an external battery pack, which can easily attach to the headset for additional power on the go.

With these tips in mind, your Meta Quest 3 gaming experience will reach new heights, allowing you to fully immerse yourself in a world of gaming possibilities. Whether you're a beginner enjoying the simplicity of user-friendly games or a seasoned VR veteran conquering advanced challenge, optimizing your experience ensures that you get the most out of every gaming session.

CHAPTER 5: PRODUCTIVITY AND BEYOND

The Meta Quest 3 has established itself as more than just a gaming device; its potential for enhancing productivity and offering new ways of working and collaborating is immense. Virtual reality in the workplace has seen significant growth, with businesses of all sizes embracing VR technology for virtual meetings, training, and team collaboration. The Quest 3, with its powerful processing capabilities and immersive design, takes these applications to a whole new level.

In the realm of virtual meetings, the Meta Quest 3 enables an entirely new way to conduct professional interactions. With applications like Horizon Workrooms, you can attend meetings in a fully immersive virtual space, where colleagues from around the world can meet, discuss, and collaborate as though they were physically in the same room. This eliminates the limitations of traditional video calls, offering a more engaging and dynamic way to interact. Whether it's brainstorming ideas on a virtual whiteboard, presenting complex data on a shared screen, or simply having a more fluid conversation, the Quest 3 transforms remote meetings into interactive experiences that can improve communication and productivity.

For training and development, VR offers unparalleled opportunities to simulate real-world scenarios without the risk or cost of traditional training methods. Whether it's teaching employees complex machinery operations or providing healthcare professionals with virtual patients for practice, VR allows individuals to practice and refine their skills in a safe, controlled environment. With the Quest 3's enhanced graphics and processing power, simulations are more detailed and realistic than ever before, creating an engaging learning experience that is far more effective than traditional methods.

Collaboration is also taken to the next level with VR, as it enables teams to work together in virtual spaces. Applications like Engage and Spatial allow for shared work environments where team members can interact with 3D models, access shared documents, and contribute to projects in real-time, all within an immersive virtual world. The ability to communicate naturally in these spaces, using body language and voice interactions, fosters a level of collaboration that far exceeds what is possible with standard video conferencing.

Beyond productivity, the Meta Quest 3 offers a wealth of creative applications that cater to a variety of artistic and developmental needs. VR has become a powerful tool for artists and designers, offering a completely new medium in which to express themselves. With tools like Tilt Brush (now part of the Google Tilt Brush suite) and Oculus Medium, users can create 3D art that surrounds them in virtual space. These applications allow for complete freedom of movement, enabling creators to sculpt, paint, and design in ways that would be impossible with traditional tools.

Designers can use the Meta Quest 3 to visualize concepts in 3D before committing to real-world production. From architectural plans to product prototypes, VR allows for instant feedback and the ability to make adjustments in real-time, providing an immersive design process. For developers, the Quest 3 provides a robust environment for creating applications and games, with access to cutting-edge development tools and the ability to test projects directly within the virtual world. This makes the Quest 3 not just a tool for consuming content, but a platform for creating it as well.

For those looking to use VR to enhance their fitness and wellness, the Meta Quest 3 provides an excellent selection of applications that support both physical activity and mental health. VR offers an innovative way to stay fit by transforming workouts into fun, engaging experiences. Apps like Supernatural and Beat Saber encourage movement while offering a fun way to exercise. Whether you're performing cardio through rhythm-based games or engaging in more traditional fitness routines, the Quest 3 makes staying active an enjoyable and immersive experience.

Fitness in VR goes beyond just cardio. Apps like FitXR provide a variety of workout types, from boxing to yoga, all in a virtual environment. These apps offer guided workouts with real-time feedback, tracking your progress and helping you stay motivated. The immersive nature of VR also means that your attention is fully captured, making it easier to stick to your routine and enjoy your workouts.

Mental wellness is another area where VR can make a significant impact, and the Meta Quest 3 has a growing library of apps designed to promote relaxation, mindfulness, and stress reduction. Apps like Tripp and Nature Treks VR offer guided meditation sessions, calming environments, and mindfulness exercises that help users manage stress and improve their mental well-being. Whether you're looking for a short mental break during a busy workday or a longer session to unwind after a challenging day, these VR applications create immersive, therapeutic experiences that are highly effective in improving mental health.

The combination of physical fitness and mental wellness in VR on the Meta Quest 3 offers a holistic approach to well-being. By engaging both the body and mind, VR can help users lead healthier, more balanced lives. With immersive environments and engaging apps that keep you motivated, the Quest 3 is a powerful tool for those looking to improve their fitness and mental state in a fun, interactive way.

In conclusion, the Meta Quest 3 has evolved beyond its gaming roots, becoming a versatile tool for work, creativity, and wellness. Whether you're using it for virtual meetings, developing cutting-edge designs, engaging in fitness challenges, or exploring mindfulness techniques, the Quest 3 offers a wealth of possibilities that go far beyond simple entertainment. With its powerful hardware, intuitive design, and expansive ecosystem of apps, the Meta Quest 3 is truly transforming how we work, create, and live.

CHAPTER 6: CUSTOMIZATION AND PERSONALIZATION

The Meta Quest 3 offers an unparalleled degree of customization, allowing users to tailor both the hardware and software to suit their individual preferences and needs. With a range of accessories and software options available, you can enhance your overall experience, whether it's optimizing comfort, boosting performance, or creating unique virtual spaces that reflect your personal style. Customization is key to making the Quest 3 truly your own, allowing you to enjoy a more comfortable and immersive journey through the metaverse.

When it comes to enhancing the hardware, there are several accessories that can take your Meta Quest 3 experience to the next level. One of the most significant upgrades is the head strap. While the standard strap is functional, many users opt for an elite strap for increased comfort and stability. The elite strap, often padded and with a more ergonomic design, reduces the pressure on the head and provides a more balanced fit, making longer VR sessions more enjoyable. Additionally, some head straps come with added features like built-in battery packs, which extend your playtime without the need for frequent recharging.

Charging docks are another excellent accessory that simplifies your charging routine. Rather than dealing with tangled cables or taking time to plug in your device each time, a charging dock offers a sleek, organized solution. It allows you to dock your Meta Quest 3 and its controllers in one place, ensuring that everything is fully charged and ready to go when you need it. Some charging stations even come with additional features, such as built-in cooling systems to keep your headset from overheating, or indicator lights to show the charging status of each device.

If you want to enhance your VR experience with improved sound, external audio solutions such as over-ear headphones or the official Quest 3 audio strap can make a huge difference. The built-in speakers of the Meta Quest 3 are decent, but the immersive experience is taken to new heights with high-quality audio accessories that deliver clearer, richer sound and better spatial audio. These accessories also add comfort, as they can eliminate the need for additional cords while still providing excellent audio quality.

Beyond hardware, the Meta Quest 3 offers a range of software customizations that allow you to personalize the way you interact with the device. Display settings are one of the first things you'll want to adjust for comfort and clarity. The Quest 3 comes with a range of options to tweak the brightness, contrast, and resolution to suit your personal preference. This is especially important if you're sensitive to screen brightness or looking to reduce eye strain during long sessions. You can also adjust the field of view settings to match your preferences, ensuring that the VR world feels as natural as possible.

Another critical software adjustment is the controller settings. The Meta Quest 3 supports a variety of controls, from traditional hand controllers to more advanced options like hand tracking. You can easily swap between different input methods depending on your preferences or the type of experience you're engaging in. Customizing the controllers involves adjusting the button mappings, sensitivity, and even activating the haptic feedback to enhance the sense of immersion. For some games, you might prefer a specific controller setup, while for others, hand tracking might be the most intuitive method. The flexibility of the Meta Quest 3 allows you to make these adjustments seamlessly.

The personal profiles feature on the Quest 3 also plays a significant role in personalizing your VR experience. By setting up individual profiles for different users, you can ensure that each person's settings, preferences, and gaming progress are kept separate. This is especially useful for families or shared households, as each user can have a customized experience without interfering with someone else's data. Personal profiles also sync across your Meta account, meaning you can easily access your saved games, preferences, and settings on any compatible Meta device, providing a truly seamless experience across the ecosystem.

Creating and designing your own virtual space is another exciting way to personalize the Meta Quest 3 experience. The Quest 3 allows you to craft home environments and virtual offices that serve as your personal retreat or working hub within the metaverse. Whether you want a tranquil environment for relaxation, a stylish workspace for meetings, or an interactive space for socializing, the possibilities are nearly limitless.

Home environments are customizable within the Quest 3 interface, where you can choose from a range of pre-designed themes or create one from scratch. This might include choosing virtual furniture, decorating with artwork or memorabilia, or adjusting the lighting to suit your mood. For example, you might create a cozy living room by the beach or a futuristic space with sleek, minimalistic furniture. These environments can also be used as a backdrop for multiplayer sessions, adding a personal touch to virtual gatherings.

In addition to personal home environments, virtual offices can be designed for professional workspaces. Whether you're using the Quest 3 for business meetings, collaboration, or creative work, you can set up a virtual office that mimics a real-world environment, or you can opt for a more futuristic or creative space that enhances focus and productivity. Customizing the layout of your virtual office can include adding screens for multitasking, integrating work tools like virtual whiteboards, and even setting up virtual desk organizers.

There are also platforms like Horizon Workrooms that allow you to create tailored virtual workspaces, with customizable elements that ensure you're comfortable and productive. You can invite colleagues into these spaces, allowing you to interact and collaborate just as you would in a physical office, with the added bonus of customizable settings to match your preferences.

Creating these virtual spaces offers more than just aesthetic satisfaction; it also plays a key role in enhancing productivity and relaxation. Your virtual environment can have a direct impact on your focus, mood, and creativity. Whether you're designing a calm escape for meditation or a dynamic office environment for brainstorming sessions, personalizing your space adds an extra layer of comfort and immersion that enhances your overall VR experience.

In conclusion, the Meta Quest 3 offers a remarkable degree of customization that extends beyond simple settings adjustments. From enhancing the physical comfort of the device with accessories like head straps and charging docks to tailoring the software for better control and display, you can create a truly personalized experience. Adding virtual spaces to the mix further elevates your immersion, allowing you to design home environments and workspaces that reflect your unique personality and needs. Customization is one of the key factors that make the Meta Quest 3 not only a powerful tool for entertainment and work but also a platform that adapts to and grows with its users.

CHAPTER 7:
TROUBLESHOOTING AND
MAINTENANCE

Owning and using a Meta Quest 3 can be an incredibly rewarding experience, but like any piece of technology, there are occasional hurdles and maintenance needs that come with regular use. Understanding how to address common issues, properly care for your device, and ensure your security while navigating the virtual world will not only help you enjoy a seamless experience but also extend the lifespan of your Meta Quest 3.

One of the most common issues users face is connectivity problems. Whether it's difficulty connecting to Wi-Fi, issues with Bluetooth, or poor internet speeds affecting your experience, these problems can often be resolved through simple troubleshooting steps. If your Meta Quest 3 is not connecting to your Wi-Fi network, the first thing you should check is your internet connection. Ensure that your router is functioning properly and that other devices are able to connect without issue. If the connection is fine on other devices, try restarting both your router and your Meta Quest 3 to refresh the network connection. Another helpful tip is to make sure your Wi-Fi signal is strong in the area where you're using the headset. Sometimes, simply moving closer to your router or using a 5GHz network can make a noticeable difference in the quality of the connection.

Tracking issues can also arise, particularly with the hand controllers or the headset's position in space. If you notice that the controllers are not being tracked accurately, or if the headset seems to be drifting in the virtual world, it might be a result of improper lighting or obstructions in the play area. To fix this, make sure that your environment has good lighting, as the Quest 3 relies on external cameras to track your movements. Avoid placing objects between the cameras and your play area, and make sure that your controllers are visible to the sensors. In some cases, recalibrating the tracking can help resolve any inconsistencies. This can be done through the settings menu, where you can reset the guardian boundary system and recalibrate the controllers to regain more accurate tracking.

Another issue that some users experience is app crashes or performance slowdowns. These issues can often be caused by outdated software, corrupted app files, or insufficient system resources. The first step in addressing app crashes is to ensure that both your Meta Quest 3's firmware and the apps you are using are up to date. Updates often include bug fixes and performance enhancements that can resolve many issues. If the problem persists, try restarting the headset to clear out any temporary bugs that may have occurred during the session. If specific apps continue to crash, it might help to uninstall and reinstall them to remove any corrupted files. For long-term maintenance, regularly clearing up storage space on your device can also help it perform at its best.

In addition to troubleshooting software and connectivity issues, regular cleaning and maintenance of your Meta Quest 3 will help preserve its condition and performance. Proper cleaning is essential to keep the device functioning optimally and to prevent any damage to sensitive components like the lenses and the sensors. Begin by gently wiping the headset's lenses with a microfiber cloth to remove any dust, fingerprints, or smudges that might affect the clarity of the image. Never use harsh cleaning chemicals or abrasive materials, as they could scratch or damage the lenses. For the rest of the headset, you can use a slightly damp cloth to wipe down the exterior. Make sure to dry the device thoroughly to avoid any moisture buildup.

The controllers also require regular cleaning, especially since they come into direct contact with your hands during use. Sweat and dirt can accumulate on the grips and buttons, so it's a good idea to wipe them down after each use. Use a soft, damp cloth to clean the controllers, and make sure they are completely dry before storing them. If the controllers become sticky or unresponsive over time, you might want to inspect the battery compartments for any dirt or debris that might have accumulated. Keep the battery contacts clean to ensure a solid connection.

Beyond simple cleaning, charging your Meta Quest 3 and controllers properly is crucial to their longevity. Avoid letting the battery completely drain regularly, as lithium-ion batteries last longer when charged before reaching very low levels. Similarly, overcharging can also reduce the lifespan of the battery, so unplugging your device once it reaches 100% is a good practice. For those who prefer an organized charging setup, using a charging dock will not only keep your devices neatly stored but also ensure they are charging safely and efficiently.

When it comes to protecting your device, it's important to consider the security measures necessary to safeguard your

Meta Quest 3. The virtual world can be a fun and interactive place, but it's equally important to stay secure while navigating it. One of the first things you should do is ensure that your Meta account is protected by a strong, unique password. Avoid using common passwords, and consider enabling two-factor authentication (2FA) for an extra layer of security. This will require you to verify your identity through a secondary device whenever you log in, making it more difficult for someone else to gain unauthorized access to your account.

You should also familiarize yourself with the privacy settings within the Meta Quest 3, as they allow you to control who can access your data and how your information is used. The Meta Quest 3 comes with various options to control your social interactions, including who can send you invites, messages, or view your activity feed. You can adjust these settings to ensure that your experience is private and secure, giving you peace of mind while exploring virtual spaces. If you're concerned about being tracked or your location being shared, review the location and data-sharing settings within the app and adjust them to your comfort level.

One of the key features of the Meta Quest 3 is the ability to create a guardian boundary for your play area, which not only protects your physical space from obstacles but also acts as a safety feature in virtual environments. It's essential to set up your guardian boundary properly to avoid accidents and to ensure that your device doesn't accidentally track movements outside of your designated play area. This feature can be recalibrated at any time, and it's a good practice to review it periodically to ensure your space remains secure.

Finally, staying secure in multiplayer and online experiences is a crucial aspect of VR use. The Meta Quest 3 allows for social interaction within virtual environments, whether through games, virtual hangouts, or work meetings. To ensure your safety, always be mindful of the people you interact with, and use the available privacy settings to manage who can contact you or join your virtual spaces. You should also be cautious of third-party apps or services that might not have the same level of security as Meta's official offerings. Stick to trusted sources for apps and games to minimize the risk of exposing yourself to potential security vulnerabilities.

In conclusion, maintaining and securing your Meta Quest 3 is essential for ensuring a seamless, enjoyable experience.

Troubleshooting common issues like connectivity problems, tracking inaccuracies, and app crashes can be done easily with the right knowledge and tools. Regular cleaning of your device and controllers will help prolong their lifespan, while proper charging practices will keep the battery in top condition. Finally, staying secure in the virtual world is just as important as physical maintenance, and taking the time to adjust privacy settings and protect your Meta account will allow you to enjoy your immersive experience with peace of mind. By following these maintenance tips and security practices, you can ensure that your Meta Quest 3 remains in excellent working condition, providing you with countless hours of entertainment, work, and creative exploration.

CHAPTER 8: DEVELOPING FOR META QUEST 3

Developing for the Meta Quest 3 opens up exciting opportunities for creators, entrepreneurs, and developers to engage with the rapidly growing world of virtual reality. Whether you're interested in creating games, apps, or immersive experiences, the Meta Quest 3 provides a robust platform for developing cutting-edge VR content. Understanding the basics of VR development, the tools and resources available to you, and the opportunities for monetization will help set you on a path to success in the immersive world of Meta Quest 3 development.

The first step in diving into VR development is understanding the basics of VR app development. Virtual reality development involves creating immersive environments that respond to the user's actions in real-time. The primary objective is to design a world where users can interact naturally and intuitively. VR development can seem complex at first, but there are a range of beginner-friendly tools and tutorials that make it accessible to developers at all levels. You don't need to be an expert in 3D modeling or game engines to get started, but a basic understanding of coding, design principles, and how VR works will be incredibly helpful.

One of the most widely used game engines for VR development is Unity, which is known for its user-friendly interface and vast library of assets and plugins. Unity also integrates well with the Meta Quest 3's software, allowing developers to quickly prototype and build VR applications. The engine's flexibility means you can develop both 2D and 3D applications, but for VR, you'll focus on the 3D aspects of the engine, working with spatial audio, physics, and immersive environments. Unreal Engine is another popular choice, known for its high-quality visuals and cinematic capabilities, making it an excellent option for developers looking to create visually stunning experiences. Both Unity and Unreal Engine have vast online communities, tutorials, and templates specifically for VR development, making it easier for new developers to get started.

In addition to game engines, developers also need access to VR-specific development tools that help bring their ideas to life. These tools are designed to simplify common tasks like interaction design, movement within virtual environments, and VR-specific user interfaces. For example, Oculus SDK

(Software Development Kit) provides a suite of tools designed specifically for Meta Quest 3 and its predecessors. These include the Oculus Integration for Unity, which offers pre-built assets, scripts, and configurations tailored to Meta's VR hardware. Similarly, the Oculus SDK for Unreal provides tools for Unreal Engine developers, with everything needed to create rich, immersive experiences for Meta devices.

Understanding how to use these tools effectively is key to successful VR development. The Oculus SDK offers functionalities like hand tracking, spatial audio, and controller support, all of which are essential for developing interactive experiences. The SDK also includes resources for optimizing performance, such as features that help you test and fine-tune the frame rate, reduce latency, and create a smooth user experience that minimizes motion sickness. These tools also allow you to implement features like passthrough mode, which integrates the real world into VR by showing a video feed from the headset's cameras. This feature is particularly useful in applications that require a blend of virtual and physical worlds, like fitness apps or augmented reality experiences.

Meta's Developer Resources are crucial for anyone looking to build for the Meta Quest 3. Meta offers extensive documentation, tutorials, and sample code to help developers get started with VR development. Accessing these resources is essential, as they provide guidance on everything from basic app creation to optimizing performance for VR. Developers can visit the official Meta developer website, where they can download SDKs, view technical documentation, and learn about the latest features supported by the Meta Quest 3. Meta's Developer Hub is a centralized platform where developers can access a variety of tutorials, join forums, and collaborate with other creators. This is a great resource for troubleshooting common problems, asking questions, and discovering new development tools.

Beyond the SDKs and APIs, Meta also provides developer events and workshops that allow you to deepen your understanding of VR development. These events often include live Q&A sessions with experienced developers, demos of new features, and opportunities to showcase your work. Meta's community-driven approach allows developers to stay updated with the latest VR trends, tools, and best practices. By leveraging these resources, you can ensure that you're creating high-quality, well-optimized VR content for Meta Quest 3 users.

As a developer, the opportunities for growth and monetization are immense. The Meta Quest Store offers a marketplace where developers can publish their apps and games, making them accessible to millions of Meta Quest users around the world. The Quest Store is one of the most widely used platforms for VR apps, with a growing user base looking for new and exciting experiences. For developers, the platform provides a powerful tool for reaching a global audience, but it's important to note that publishing on the store requires adherence to Meta's guidelines and approval process. This means ensuring your app is fully optimized for performance, has an engaging user experience, and complies with content policies.

Monetizing VR apps can be done through several channels, with the most common being paid apps and in-app purchases. Developers can choose to charge a one-time fee for their app, allowing users to purchase and access the full experience. Alternatively, in-app purchases offer a more flexible model, where users can download the app for free and make purchases for additional content, features, or upgrades within the app. Another monetization option is the subscription model, which allows users to access exclusive content or experiences on an ongoing basis. By offering regular updates, exclusive experiences, or premium content, developers can create a recurring revenue stream from their apps.

Meta also provides developers with the opportunity to participate in various partnerships and promotional programs that can help expand their reach. For example, developers can participate in Meta's App Lab program, which allows apps to be featured and promoted through Meta's marketing channels. These programs are a great way for developers to gain exposure and attract new users, especially if they are just starting out or have a niche app that may not fit into the traditional Quest Store catalog. Developers can also collaborate with Meta on promotions, discounts, or special events to drive more attention to their apps.

One of the key aspects of developing for Meta Quest 3 is understanding the importance of user feedback. Since VR is an immersive, interactive medium, users' reactions to your app or game are vital for improving its design and functionality. Gathering feedback from early adopters, beta testers, and the broader community will help you make necessary adjustments before launching your app to a wider audience. Meta's platform also provides analytics tools that allow you to track how users are engaging with your app, including which features are the most popular, where users are spending the most time, and where they might be dropping off. This data can help guide your development efforts and fine-tune your app for the best possible user experience.

In addition to developing games and experiences for entertainment, there is also a growing demand for enterprise applications in the VR space. The Meta Quest 3 is increasingly being used for business purposes, such as training, collaboration, and remote work. This opens up a wealth of opportunities for developers interested in creating VR apps for productivity and enterprise solutions. VR has proven to be an effective tool for remote meetings, interactive training simulations, and virtual collaboration in design and engineering. As the demand for virtual workspaces continues to rise, developers who focus on creating innovative tools for businesses will find themselves at the forefront of this burgeoning industry.

In conclusion, developing for Meta Quest 3 offers vast opportunities for creators across various industries, from gaming to enterprise solutions. By understanding the basics of VR development and leveraging Meta's extensive developer resources, you can create immersive, interactive experiences that captivate users. The potential for monetization and reaching a global audience through the Meta Quest Store further incentivizes developers to build high-quality VR applications. Whether you're an aspiring VR developer or an experienced creator, Meta Quest 3 provides the tools, resources, and opportunities to succeed in the rapidly evolving world of virtual reality.

CHAPTER 9: THE FUTURE OF VR AND META QUEST 3

As virtual reality continues to evolve, the future of VR and devices like the Meta Quest 3 is incredibly exciting. Innovations in artificial intelligence, 5G technology, and the ongoing development of the Metaverse are all paving the way for more immersive, connected, and intelligent VR experiences. Understanding how these emerging technologies will influence VR is essential for anyone invested in the future of virtual reality, whether as a user, developer, or tech enthusiast.

One of the most significant technological advancements shaping the future of VR is the integration of artificial intelligence (AI). AI is not just transforming VR in terms of how experiences are created but also in how users interact with the virtual world. Machine learning algorithms enable VR systems to become more adaptive and responsive to the individual behaviors of users. For instance, AI can enhance the realism of interactions by predicting user movements or creating more dynamic environments that evolve based on the user's choices. AI is also improving the way VR applications are built by offering more intelligent systems for procedural content generation, such as creating unique landscapes or

NPCs (non-playable characters) with more lifelike behaviors. The integration of AI-driven systems within VR has the potential to create personalized, ever-changing virtual worlds that adapt in real time, making every experience feel fresh and tailored.

Furthermore, 5G technology is playing a critical role in the future of VR, particularly when it comes to wireless experiences. The Meta Quest 3, like its predecessors, is a standalone VR headset, meaning it doesn't need to be tethered to a PC or console to function. However, the device's potential is amplified when combined with 5G networks, which offer ultra-fast internet speeds and low latency. This technology will enable cloud-based VR, where users can access complex, high-fidelity VR experiences without the need for powerful local hardware. 5G will also reduce the lag in VR interactions, ensuring that real-time movements and actions in virtual environments feel instantaneous, which is crucial for creating immersive and natural experiences. The synergy between AI and 5G will revolutionize VR by allowing users to experience more dynamic, interactive, and seamless content without any interruptions or delays, transforming the way we interact with virtual spaces.

As Meta continues to innovate in the realm of VR, its long-term goal is centered around the development of the Metaverse—a vast, interconnected virtual universe where users can work, socialize, create, and experience content in new and immersive ways. The Metaverse is envisioned as the next phase of the internet, a space where the lines between the physical and virtual worlds blur, and users can engage with each other through avatars in shared virtual spaces. For Meta, the Quest 3 is more than just a VR headset—it's a gateway to this expansive Metaverse, which Meta sees as a platform that will drive the next generation of social interactions, entertainment, and business. The Quest 3's advanced mixed reality features, like passthrough and hand tracking, are stepping stones towards creating more integrated and lifelike virtual environments. These features will help Meta's vision of the Metaverse come to life by making virtual spaces feel more connected to the real world, allowing for richer, more meaningful experiences.

The Metaverse is not just about entertainment—it has the potential to revolutionize how we interact socially. In the Metaverse, users can attend virtual events, collaborate in shared workspaces, and build relationships with people from all over the world. Meta's long-term vision includes virtual spaces that simulate real-world activities like shopping, learning, or collaborating on projects, all from the comfort of your own home. One of the primary goals is to create more immersive environments where users don't just consume content but actively participate and shape the experience. Whether it's hosting a meeting in a virtual office, attending a concert with friends, or exploring a digitally recreated city, the Metaverse is designed to offer limitless possibilities for social interaction and connectivity.

The quest to create these immersive experiences doesn't stop with entertainment and socialization. Meta envisions the Metaverse as a new frontier for evolution in social interactions—changing how we communicate, build relationships, and even work. Instead of simply chatting via text or video calls, the Metaverse would allow users to meet in virtual spaces, walk through shared environments, and interact in real-time with more natural gestures and movements. This is where Meta Quest 3's advanced features like eye-tracking, spatial audio, and hand gestures come into play, as they provide the building blocks for a more natural and engaging form of communication. By integrating these technologies, Meta aims to create virtual environments where human interactions feel intuitive and authentic, making virtual socializing more fulfilling than ever before.

For businesses, the Metaverse is poised to become a game-changer, providing a new medium for collaboration, innovation, and customer engagement. Virtual workspaces could replace traditional office settings, enabling people to work together in a more dynamic and flexible way. Imagine collaborating on a design project where every team member is immersed in a shared virtual space, manipulating 3D models and offering feedback in real-time, no matter where they are located. Virtual meetings will become more engaging and efficient, and team-building activities could even take place in gamified environments that promote creativity and communication. Meta Quest 3, with its ability to create lifelike avatars and interactive spaces, is laying the groundwork for this type of work environment in the future.

As we look ahead, the Meta Quest 3 is part of a broader tech landscape that is rapidly evolving. Virtual reality itself is transforming, and its integration with AI, 5G, and the Metaverse shows that the possibilities for VR applications are endless. From immersive entertainment and gaming to enterprise solutions and social collaboration, Meta Quest 3 is at the center of this revolution, providing a platform for users to experience the next generation of virtual environments.

Meta's continued focus on innovation and integration with emerging technologies positions the Quest 3 as more than just a gaming device—it's a powerful tool for accessing the future of digital interactions. As AI advances, we will likely see smarter and more personalized experiences, whether for entertainment, education, or professional collaboration. Similarly, the growth of 5G networks will allow for an unprecedented level of connectivity, enabling more people to access high-quality VR experiences with minimal barriers. And as Meta's vision for the Metaverse comes to fruition, the Meta Quest 3 will play an integral role in bridging the gap between the physical and virtual worlds, offering an immersive gateway for all users to participate in this exciting new era.

The Meta Quest 3 is not just a device; it is the bridge between today's world and the immersive, interconnected future. With AI, 5G, and the Metaverse at the forefront of Meta's vision, the Quest 3 will continue to evolve, shaping the way we experience the digital world and redefining the boundaries of what's possible. Whether for entertainment, education, work, or social interaction, the Meta Quest 3 stands as a testament to the exciting potential that lies ahead in the world of virtual reality. As we prepare for what's next, the future of VR promises to be more immersive, engaging, and connected than ever before.

EPILOGUE

Reflecting on your journey with the Meta Quest 3, it becomes clear that this is not just a device—it's an entirely new way to experience and interact with the digital world. As you've discovered throughout this book, the Quest 3 offers more than just immersive gaming; it opens up an array of possibilities that extend into productivity, creativity, wellness, and social interaction. The device allows you to step into entirely new worlds, connect with people across the globe, create something unique, and experience entertainment in ways that were once unimaginable. Whether you're a beginner or an experienced user, the Meta Quest 3 empowers you to redefine what it means to be connected to technology, offering an immersive, boundary-pushing experience that adapts to your needs.

Making the most of your Meta Quest 3 means embracing the full potential of what VR has to offer. Begin by exploring the vast library of experiences, from casual games to sophisticated applications that push the boundaries of what you thought possible. Take time to familiarize yourself with the features, from hand tracking to passthrough, and learn how they can enhance your interactions. As you gain more experience, consider how you can personalize your virtual spaces, adjust settings for comfort, and dive deeper into social features, allowing you to make meaningful connections in the virtual world. The Meta Quest 3 provides tools that allow you to tailor your VR experience to your preferences, whether you're gaming, collaborating on a project, or simply relaxing in a virtual environment.

The key to truly enjoying the Meta Quest 3 is staying curious and open to new experiences. There's no right or wrong way to use the device—what matters most is how it enhances your life. Don't hesitate to experiment with new apps, explore different genres of VR content, or even develop your own VR creations. The future of VR is still unfolding, and as technology continues to advance, your Meta Quest 3 will continue to evolve alongside it. Keeping an open mind and a sense of wonder is essential in fully appreciating what this device has to offer.

As you journey further into the world of VR, you'll find that a world of possibilities awaits. The Meta Quest 3 is just the beginning. From virtual fitness experiences that promote physical health and wellness to professional training programs that transform how we work, VR is a tool for change and innovation. It's an invitation to create, explore, and redefine your understanding of what's possible in both the virtual and real worlds. Whether you're seeking entertainment, self-improvement, or simply an escape from reality, the Meta Quest 3 offers something for everyone.

The future of virtual reality is incredibly bright, and it's exciting to think about where it will take us. As the technology behind VR continues to improve, Meta's Quest devices will evolve to offer even more dynamic, realistic, and engaging experiences. The introduction of AI, 5G, and the Metaverse will expand the ways we interact with the world around us, bringing people closer together and making the impossible a reality. The Meta Quest 3 is your gateway into this future—an immersive tool that empowers you to explore new ideas, interact with a vibrant global community, and create experiences that resonate with both you and others.

By taking full advantage of the possibilities available to you, you're not just a passive participant in VR—you're an active creator, explorer, and innovator. The virtual spaces you explore, the games you play, and the apps you develop can all be a part of a broader movement to push the boundaries of what technology can do. In this sense, the Meta Quest 3 serves as more than just a device—it's an invitation to be part of something much larger, something that is continually evolving and offering new opportunities for growth and exploration.

As you continue to make the most of your Meta Quest 3, remember that VR is about expanding your horizons. The world of possibilities is vast, and with the Meta Quest 3, you're just beginning to scratch the surface. So, whether you're taking your first steps into the virtual world or diving deeper into your VR journey, keep pushing the limits of what's possible. The future of VR, and your place within it, is just waiting to be discovered. With curiosity, creativity, and an adventurous spirit, you're bound to find endless opportunities for enjoyment, learning, and innovation. The Meta Quest 3 is your tool to create, explore, and experience the world in ways that were once only imagined. Embrace the adventure—there's no telling where it will take you.